THE END OF THE PIER SHOW

By the same author

Living Room
From the Other Country
Over the Wall
Out for the Elements
Selected Poems
In the Planetarium

anthology

The Poetry of Chess

Andrew Waterman

The End of the Pier Show

CARCANET

First published in 1995 by
Carcanet Press Limited
402-406 Corn Exchange Buildings
Manchester M4 3BY

A CIP catalogue record for this book
is available from the British Library
ISBN 1 85754 221 5

The publisher acknowledges financial assistance
from the Arts Council of England

Set in 10 pt Palatino by Bryan Williamson, Frome
Printed and bound in England by SRP Ltd, Exeter

Acknowledgements

Acknowledgements are due to the editors of the following, in which many of these poems first appeared: *Critical Quarterly, London Magazine, PN Review, Poetry Review, The Spectator*.

Contents

Uncle Bob

'Use your feet, and bring the bat down true
To the line of flight, head down, and Bob's your uncle!'
They said; or maybe, 'Think the problem through,
Tackle it stage by stage, and Bob's your uncle!'

Meaning it will be fine, turn out all right.
Having no Uncle Bob, I'd fantasise
A puissant lordly being out of sight,
Monitoring my every enterprise.

His hands on all the ropes, and never lost
For a solution, supernatural kin,
Concerned, however we felt mauled and tossed
By life, to see us right, through thick and thin.

Years brought wrong choices, people, home to stay.
For others, too. Unsolvable. Had Bob
Lost touch, not known his work fall miles astray,
Or flushed with the high life dozed off on the job?

No – not remotely all we'd cracked him up
To be, just a quixotic simpleton,
Even before he finally cracked up
Under the drift of things, he'd never won

A major title, steered the ship of state,
Or written Tolstoy. Now he's on his uppers,
Outcast, derided, an old reprobate
Scavenging bins for remnants of fish suppers.

Still meaning well, and wishing others joy.
From the corner of a pub he tips a wink,
Seeing again Miss Right meet the wrong boy,
Smiles 'Bob's your uncle!' raising his cadged drink.

Paper Boats

I roam the *Contents* pages, look to see
Who's in, who's out. More women these days. So,
A lot here born a fair while after me,
And some of even these, I notice . . . No,
At least I'm not tagged with a terminal date:
Still *1940 -* . The anthology falls
Closed. Though not being dead yet seems no great
Reason for being alive. Then that appals
Me – catching myself thinking what I know
I'd never have thirty, or ten, years ago.

So what's occurred, what changes? Well, it's not
Shrivelling passions or intensities
Or lyric feelings, all intact. But what
Form like a glow, as clear transparencies,
Are pictures: the lit Thames from a midnight train
Grinding across a railbridge; pools of white
Pavement petals hushing footfall; rain
Golden in lamplight past my window; bright
Primary colours strewn on beaches; and
The blare and glitter from a park bandstand.

When Cowdrey drove through mid-off, seaside piers
Had What-the-Butler-Saw machines, politics
Was pure crusade to end 'the wasted years' . . .
The potency is more than heady tricks
Of gulped nostalgia. Adrift from schooling, home,
I scribbled novel-drafts, joked how I might
Yet rake in middle-distance golds, or comb
Far space for cosmic secrets, move a knight
To clinch the world chess crown. So much lay before me,
Including the glorious girls – could not ignore me.

Or further back: a fragile glint and dance
Of dragonflies over pond; print on my palm
Of bracken where I'd leant; a morning trance
Absorbing patterns of grain on a chair-arm...
Moments our rest-of-life becomes a quest
In some form to transcribe, all sealed away
In past we're exiled from, defines it best –
Now I've *got it made* the world would say...
Ahead, the paper boats I and my son
Launch, vanish into tunnel, one by one.

'The Beautiful Game'

(Pele)

for Nanette Dotterweich

This summer's drained of vivid promises,
A chill negation of what should have been;
Betrayed from which, I slump among what is,
Watch World Cup football flicker on my screen.
It too falls short, squanders in dreariness,
Unjust results, gifts thwarted, patternless.
Useless in memory glow Pele's sway
Dummying that goalie, ghost-glides of Tostao.
Yet like life too this game will never fail
Us quite, slips leaden days by alchemising
From battle to romance: that through-pass now,
A juggling run, the net shakes, and I'm rising
To beauty opened like a peacock's tail.

1990

Tenby

Free of life's wastage
The name sounded clear:
Tenby, a bell's
Double chime in my ear.

But when we arrived
Tenby fell into place,
Now configured precisely
Within time and space,

Its cliff-gardens dropping
To a curve of gold sand,
Small harbour, old watchtower
On a high jut of land.

Ah, Dynbych-y-Pysgod,
'Little fort of the fishes',
The postcards we filled
With holiday wishes

Showed once-guarded town walls,
And Pembrokeshire's vast
Hunks of castle where brood
Bloody deeds of the past.

And twice daily the tide
Cut off Goscar Rock,
And nothing could halt
The whirl of the clock...

When it slid from our train
I was glad of our few
Days in Tenby, redeemed
From transcendent to true;

Of our walk fluctuating
From forest to cliff,
Our boat to the island,
The jokes we shared. If

My son as you splashed
In the waves all the cries
Arising seemed tiny,
Brief under the sky's

Huge arch as the vanished
Clamour of strife
Among Normans, Welsh, English,
Still through your life

Things you gazed at when perched
On that cannon, or did –
Beach football, rock scrambling –
Will come back, amid

All accretions, erosions;
Ceremonious, immune.
Keynotes. To such, all
Our years reattune.

In Ward 27

'All art aspires
To the condition
Of music' . . . Yes,
But what all art utters
Is life aspiring
To solacing structure,
To purification.
So it is life
That craves to be music.

Tell that to the wearied
Brown backs of Brueghel's
Three hunters descending
The snow through stark trees:
Their cold day, the boughs'
Rigid tracery, village
Below, where children
Are sliding, redeemed
Through art's timeless vision.

Also 'words, words, words' –
None knew better than Shakespeare –
Are stuck in the mud
Of our human turmoil.
Mad Ophelia dying,
Betrayals, revenges,
Cry out unaware
Of the form they are shaped to –
Forms never rinsed clear

Of our mortal lot, here
For instance, shuffling
A corridor floor,
Counting the hours
Between cups of tea,
Till wheeled to the surgeon.
In the ophthalmic ward
The vision we crave
Is simple indeed.

Only music inhabits
That ultimate sphere
Purged of life's blemish.
It moves through abstractions.
Past reach? In a sense.
Yet, removed, I find Elgar's
Cello concerto
Proves eyes wrecked for seeing
Still buoyant with tears.

Shore Lines

'Follow the inner shore-line round the bend,'
 The social worker says, her term denoting
The wall-side of the pavement. I attend
 To 'outdoor mobility' instruction, noting
 That 'slipway' here is a far cry from boating,
Just driveways from house garages. To gaze
 Around though rather makes me feel I'm floating
Far out among suburbs hulking through a haze
I know will never clear through my remaining days.

Coming to in the ward I couldn't see
 Anything, left eye blind for years, a pad
Strapped to the other after surgery.
 I gulped the sweetest tea I've ever had,
 The nurse just voice and guiding arm. When clad
For discharge two days later, 'It's been a novel
 Experience,' I told Sister. 'Not that bad
Surely?' she bridled – hearing it as 'an awful'.
I've to relearn how to live, work, relate to people, travel.

Don't vacuum, carry shopping, wash your hair
 Read the instructions. However, I must feed
Myself, bath, keep at least indoors tidy. So
 I negotiate days slowed to tortoise speed,
 Mocked by shelves of books I cannot read,
The only social highlights pub and shopping.
 Teach literature again? My hopes recede.
Dumped in a chair, dawdling the kitchen mopping,
All I can be sure of is this never stopping

Lying in bed, when I've switched off the light,
 I tune to the Shipping Forecast's poetry:
Dogger . . . Fisher . . . Rockall . . . German Bight . . .
 Trafalgar . . . Malin . . . Visibility
 Poor with mist patches. A long litany
Conjuring, as more rain falls, evocations
 Of little vessels tossed far out at sea.
Then follows the *reports from coastal stations,*
Boomer . . . Dover . . . Mumbles . . . My imagination's

Jumped point-to-point round bays and promontories
     Of our whole shore-line, varying sweeps of sand,
Castle-topped headlands harbouring ancient stories . . .
     Weather reports for inshore waters – and
     Hearing *from Cromer to Dungeness*, I stand
With my son last spring on that eroding cliff,
     The path from Cromer round to Overstrand.
I vow, although all future scares me stiff,
We'll walk that way again, a case of when, not if.

Meanwhile I am hard-pressed to walk the street:
     The town is thronged, the entrance to each store
A social venue where people go to meet,
     Hold seminars on the October weather or
     The price of things. Do I need shinpads for
Protection against kamikaze pushchairs flying
     Towards me? Home, bags unpacked on the floor,
I find the tomatoes I'd thought I'd been buying
Are onions – they'll serve just as well for breakfast frying.

I'll never take up golf, or drive a car
     Again; art's out; so far as I can see
I may no more look for love than find a star.
     'Perhaps,' I joke, 'I'm qualified to be
     A cricket umpire, football referee.'
I'm told of various retraining courses
     By someone sent from the RNIB,
Closed-circuit TV to read by, other resources.
I sign on, ready for the jumps as any horse is.

While footbound I dodge each day's permutation
     Of scaffold-poles, dug-up paving, heaps of sand,
Concrete troughs of civic vegetation,
     Pavement-parked cars, skips jutting head-high, and
     Vans' side-mirrors. Confident I'd scanned
My familiar home streets tonight, I walked
     Thwack into something soft my clutching hand
Held from falling over as it squawked:
A dark-coated little old dear. 'I'm sorry.' Smiles; we talked.

Fastnet . . . Humber . . . Thames . . . Wight . . . Finisterre . . .
   Disease and disability are like,
I've heard, a foreign country. Exiled there,
   I whisper to a cassette recorder mike
   Memories of my native land that spike
All new resolve: landscapes I used to know,
   Where I played tennis, learned to ride a bike,
The country called health, where I can never go.
Malin Head, falling slowly . . . Tiree, continuing snow.

And all night it's the sea, successive dreams
   In which its deepest blues have flooded back.
The cretinous subconscious, bent it seems
   On plundering colour with kleptomaniac
   Avidity, denies I've lost the knack,
Must wake to a drained field of blanks and blotch,
   Each day a misty day . . . However black
The outlook, two things this can never botch:
The music of Beethoven and the taste of a good Scotch.

As always, others are far worse off than me:
   Children sightless from traffic accidents,
Or programmed to this by heredity;
   Casualties from our Ulster violence;
   The suicide attempt who aimed askance,
Condemned to life thus. Black or brown or pink,
   It's blind to that, wealth, or intelligence –
Like Cupid, as old Greeks supposed. Or drink.
We tread like fogbound walkers, ignorant to the brink.

I'm practising the keyboard skills I'll need,
   No more the old three-finger look-and-poke.
Instead of print exercises I can't read
   I use radio: *Soundtrack, Down Your Way* from Stoke;
   A cookery slot expounds the artichoke.
The social worker thinks I'll pull through fine.
   Thinking of mad Swift gesturing at an oak
Blasted by lightning, I type *Heseltine*
Looks strongest on the first ballolt, must Thatcher now resign?

She wears checks and bright colours to help clients
    See where she is; discourses on her store
Of gadgetry devised by useful science:
    Bleepers to fit a cup so you don't pour
    Your tea to overbrim and flood the floor,
Dictaphones, magnifiers, clocks you feel;
    I could hold the whole world in my hands once more
With a Braille globe, or learn to cook a meal
By touch. Aids which confirm a fate they cannot heal.

Even my eyes pick out her wedding-ring
    Across the room. 'Do you have children?' 'No.'
She's moved by talk of my son. Claims gardening
    Is her passion. In my mind rich blossoms glow,
    Fragrances infiltrate, from long ago.
'Never my line.' She talks of when flower shows start,
    And flower arranging – Michelangelo
To her a closed book, also Shakespeare, Mozart,
She thinks primping primroses, phlox, ferns and oats art.

I've flown the Irish Sea, am in a train
    Jinking across Lincolnshire to my son . . .
We stroll round the cathedral, once again
    Ascend the castle walls; I even run
    For a bus. And his concern for me is fun
As well as touching: he finds things in a shop,
    Now reads me bedtime *William* stories. Un-
derneath all which, he's weighed me up, post-op:
'I think you're managing, Dad. At least your jokes don't stop.'

'If it were only carrots that Kuwait
    Produced, not oil, the West would let Iraq
Stay put,' I argue. Faces remonstrate,
    Blurred gold as I knock the next whiskey back.
    Waking painfully from another black-
out, I wonder how on earth my feet
    Walked me home, finger a bloodied crack
On my forehead, must have fallen in the street,
Hit scaffolding. My hands are jittering as I eat.

Touch-skills now incorporate the top row,
    Numbers, tapping out changes of address
With postcodes soon gets tedious, and so
    Instead I devise what surely must, I guess,
    Be the first ever practical use for chess:
e4 c5; Nf3 d6; d4 . . .
    I play myself blindfold till the wilderness
Of variations halts me at its shore . . .
The news: *Saddam defiant as the Allies gear for war.*

I've taken down my Christmas cards today.
    The count of paces from which as I stroll
To the University I make out that GIVE WAY
    Sign's up – a trick of light. In bed I scroll
    Through last week's English holiday, on parole
From fear, guilt, doubt: the game for me, theatric-
    ally cheering as my son described each goal,
Was spot the ball. But our star scored a hat-trick.
Inshore waters . . . Calm . . . from Holyhead to Portpatrick.

Calling, she wields a saw; 'Is that to chop
    Up clients?' No, to shorten a white stick
For a lady she's en route to. 'Can you stop
    For coffee?' 'Yes.' She suddenly leans to pick
    Fluff from my shirt. I'm moved. Impolitic,
She questions my gaze . . . By now each knows the score,
    We fence, then shy love gushes from the quick,
Clasping us to each other on the floor,
Tender, salt, dangerous. As the Gulf slides to war.

Through TV it woos millions, provided
    With armchair spectacle as fireworks pluck
Out evil, and our 'smart bombs', laser-guided,
    Follow along a street, turn corners, duck
    To doff at chosen doors what blows to fuck
Flesh scraped to burial next day in Baghdad.
    'Collateral damage' screens as pure ill-luck
A blown-up school; while back here Mum and Dad
Find 'friendly fire' means John's mid-air death's not so bad.

I wake in hospital, not knowing how
   I came here or who brought me, an appalling
Headache, row of stitches in my brow.
    Drunk to the world, I don't remember falling.
    I get back home, and bath: today she's calling.
Sweating, shaking, I can hardly manage
   A tray. 'What did you have?' I'm lying, stalling.
She's angry, hurt. Thus love's collateral damage.
Land's End to Cape Wrath, fog. . . My eyes close on the image.

White canes, dogs, ghetto-jokes about meals and bruises –
   Among others on this course who've not the choice
I've magnification software. What they use is
   Perfect Percy, a synthetic voice
   That would make Tennyson sound like James Joyce.
Killing the Gulf, high-tech's benign to me:
   Word-processing, scanners, printers, audio-toys . . .
Our tanks entomb the dug-in enemy,
Oil wells flame, vast spillage clogs wildlife in dead sea.

I parch for colours that when I was a child
   My paintbox held, vermilion, cobalt blue,
Ochres and purples, as I wait in mild
   Weather past GIVE WAY, the river view
   Spread bleached beneath me. Flickering anew,
Green buds on last year's lopped boughs. Craving for
   The primary virtues, beautiful, good, true,
I take the coast bus; and strolling on the shore
Press RECORD, augmenting a cassette's unsorted store.

– Three years ago. Another spring. Reliving
   Those months I know time never can complete
Its flux of joys, loss, sorrows, bitter-sweet.
   While inhumanities we can't defeat
   Have shifted to Bosnia. Once more we meet,
I take her arm, link with my son, to crest
   Crumbling cliff against which strong tides beat;
Like Herbert trusting in, whatever test
Lies always round the bend, the 'gladness of the best'.

The Scheme of Things

1   FIRST WORLD

How it enfolds me now, that earliest world
Whispering on against the garden fence:
A leftover stretch of Epping Forest curled
Round our small garden crescent, in its dense
Thickets and bracken, sun-splashed glades, our play,
Near as my heartbeat still woodpigeons brooding,
Sudden again the blue flash of a jay.
Why should I hesitate, as if intruding?

– Who clinging high in a storm-battered tree
Once sang, 'Eternal Father, strong to save,'
The hymn 'for those in peril on the sea',
Thrilling to know joy won by being brave,
Fears simple then, unstained by guilts or failure.
Boughs creaked. When I grew up, I'd be a sailor.

2   NATURE LESSONS

My forest Eden wasn't unspoilt nature.
Older children, born before the war,
Told which ponds were true pond, which just bomb-crater.
What were those concrete fangs across it for? –
'To stop the German tanks.' In the night sky
Searchlights, bombers, droning, bangs, V2s,
Since I could remember. Pointless wondering why –
Such things were since it said so on the news.

Cows straying down our road were more amazing:
Loose in the forest, there they were one morning
Nudging at front gates, stood in flowers grazing.
And more sinister to me than air-raid warnings
Was that dank rubber in ferns, which my friend Nick
Said had been up a girl on some man's prick.

3   INTIMATIONS

Thick autumn leaves shoaled orange, gold and red
Beneath the beech, more precious than all toys.
I gathered up the choicest, pocketed
Them to keep. Next week, 'The rubbish boys,'
Guffawaed the barber, as I delved and blushed,
Finding at last my ninepence only after
Disgorging a heap of brittle shreds, brown dust,
'Stuff in their clothes!' I fled the adult laughter.

Annually frogspawn mantled every pond.
I'd scoop up dollops into jamjars, bring
Them home, for weeks watch with anticipation
Tadpoles sprout legs, so few survive beyond,
To make the next green hopping generation;
And feel betrayed by the whole scheme of things.

4   FATHER

Leant back, knees bent, eyes down, hands plunged in pockets,
Dad flipped the ball just right for me to head.
I'd wake to see beside his empty bed
Draped on the chair his office suit, the jacket
Fragrant with pipe tobacco, hear him splashing.
I stole sixpence when the shops first sold
Ice-lollies postwar, tasted a pink cold
Dissolving sweetness, fearful of a thrashing.

Yet thieved again. Until Dad must have known
But, unperturbed, still on our Sunday strolls
Chipped up the ball, named trees. He kept his tools
Gleaming and sharp; and when I asked had shown
Why the spirit-level's jittery little bubble
Should be centred, steadying it upon the table.

5 INDOORS AND OUT

Shelling peas indoors with Mum, I stared
At the line of tree-tops cresting through grey rain
Spattering our garden laurels. When it cleared
I went out to a world washed new again.
The earth released fresh smells. I stood and listened
To thrushes whistling in a hawthorn thicket,
Pressing my palm against wet bark to mark it;
Waterdrops pearled twigs where berries glistened.

Suppose a tree-house on a hidden bough:
I'd pull the rope-ladder up behind me, lose
Myself among leaves' year-long ceremonial.
'Andrew, get up!' they call, 'You're late for school.'
If I could do just anything I chose
I'd build that tree-house, and be in it now.

6 FRIENDS

First kids in our road, then friends met at school.
We vied tree-climbing, running, sometimes fought.
Nick, George Stone, Rodney Baxter, Brian who taught
Me to spell 'queueing', the Fortey twins ('Just two'll
Be quite enough') . . . From ropes above the Ching
We'd swing, let go, land safe on the far side.
Whooping along on bikes and trikes, we'd ride
To Loughton, Ilford, circles widening.

Where are they now? Some grandparents, some dead.
Passing in streets, there'd be no recognising.
In me they live forever bracketed:
Fairisle pullovers, Woolworths' snake-clasp belts,
Plaster on knees. On branches cut to stilts,
Or pedalling homeward as the moon is rising.

7 BREAK-UP

Mum moved with sister and me to the far side
Of London. My nine-years world whirled away.
Dad I heard nothing more of till he died.
Grown-up, I went back, found bits where we'd play
Gone, built over; strange toys lined the sill
Of our old house. But still my favourite beech...
I didn't climb, knew things less tangible
Than its low-slung bough were out of reach:

As if through dripping sheets of ice we'd break
From ponds we dangerously slid on when they froze;
Aqueous, refracted. Futile to revisit
What only lives within me. Though why is it
So vivid now?...Hands on the oars, Dad rows
A family on summer's trembling lake.

Then and Now

But then the heart of loneliness was light.
An attic patient for the haul I brought
Back to sort beneath the lamp each night:

Office-talk; who's marrying; or been caught
Fiddling the petty cash; the rush and scent
Of girls; upon grey city roofs at dusk

The starlings' melancholy loud descent.
Gathered, like chestnuts rolled from the shed husk,
For my great novel, comic yet heartbreaking.

Still I grew beyond it. Relationships, career,
Things take you out of yourself. Nowadays waking
Alone's sole clouded luminary is fear,

Its skies a pallor as when after snow
Has fallen gives away the blanked terrain
All round. Of what has been and will remain

Untended. Time sifts down, obliterating
Glance and gesture; the live acrid glow
Of jazz once flickering from a Soho grating.

Soap

Steve's taken to the cleaners by his wife;
Granny Grunge has a suspicious lump;
Round the King's Arms Shirl's warned big trouble's rife;
Dad's live-in girl-friend gives young Keith the hump.
And Sandra's *gorra gerrout* of this dump,
She wants to *do things, live a bit, see life.*

No chance she'll vroom off in a heliotrope
Ferrari, make the Cabinet, or Peru;
Mums brat-beset at breakfast brightly cope
Only in ads, where she'd be married too,
And magic powders wash all our dreams true.
Their lot's off-white, week in week out. It's soap.

It shifts the worst stains. Keith won't slash his throat;
The old folk never piss themselves or drivel;
Fists rock pub regulars, but not the boat.
Blacks, gays? Fine, if they come up smiling, civil.
World within world! all problems but no evil.
Poets and murderers reach for the remote.

The range pretended to is given back
Squashed. What they play is never chess or Brahms;
Granny Grunge fights off the cells' attack;
God's social detail, nothing that alarms.
Planning an IRA bomb for the King's Arms
To clear the decks, got scriptwriters the sack.

So Wayne and Duane go on both chasing Sharon.
The credits roll, *Devised by*... But who cares
Why Tracey slags off Stacey over Darren?
Rinsing off suds, we turn to our affairs,
Unscheduled, past containments or repairs;
Gloriously unplottable. Not barren.

Dora, Dick, Nip and Fluff

Here is Dora. Here is Dick. And here
Is Nip. And here is Fluff. The sun shines clear
From a blue sky. See Nip and Fluff at play.
Nip is black and white. Fluff's fur is grey.
'Woof,' says Nip. Fluff jumps up on the wall.
Here comes Dora with a bouncy ball.
How Nip romps [new word] with it. But now
Dora throws the red ball high. 'Mee-ow,'
Says Fluff, 'I think that this is meant for me.'
And look, the ball is stuck up in a tree.
'Go after it,' says Dora. See Fluff climb
To a high limb [which only *looks* a rhyme].
'Mee-ow,' says Fluff, 'I cannot get the ball.'
'Come down,' calls Dora. 'But I think I'll fall,'
Says Fluff, 'Mee-ow, mee-ow, I can't go down.'
'Oh, poor Fluff,' says Dora with a frown
[New word]. 'Woof, woof,' barks Nip, 'Let us fetch Dick.'
They go indoors, tell Dick. Dick gets a stick.
Dick runs into the garden. 'I can get
Fluff down and the ball too,' he says. 'Poor pet,'
Says Dora. Dick climbs up the tree and takes
Fluff in his arms, pokes with his stick and shakes
Until the ball drops bouncing. Soon he's got
Himself and Fluff down. Dora's so glad. 'What
Shall we play now?' she chuckles, 'Games are fun.'
They chase [new word] each other. See Nip run.
'Dick, your chum Hamie's here, for tea,' calls Mum.

But Shakespeare [new word] knew there's more to come.

I that please some, try all, both joy and terror.
Of good and bad; that makes and unfolds error,
Now take upon me, in the name of Time,
To use my wings. Impute it not a crime
To me, or my swift passage, that I glide
O'er sixteen years, and leave the growth untried . . .

See Dick, flat out on a soiled mattress, clutch
His head. He has the shakes. Dick drinks too much.
Divorce [new word and new experience]
Has fouled Dick up. 'Thank God I had the sense
Not to have kids,' Dick says. Dick's lost his job.
He puts off girls he chases. Dick's a slob.
He swigs his bedside Scotch. 'I'll make the door.'
Dick trips on something smelly on the floor.
'Grrr.' Yes, it's Nip. Poor Nip can hardly stand.
Nip has the runs. He cannot understand
The new words 'stomach tumour'. Soon he'll die
[New experience], not knowing why.

See Baby Tim clap hands in Dora's face,
Not knowing he's classed as a high-risk case
At Social Services. Tim's still too dumb
To ask why Granny's younger than his Mum.
'It's Dad's remarriage to that teenage bitch
Who paints her toenails green,' says Dora, 'which
Made me quit college.' Dora's on the game.
And heroin [no, this word's not the same
As heroine]. Prone as often as her brother,
But under some man, each just like another.
'Go after it,' says Dora, to their shoving
Buttocks. She tells Dick, 'I'm just fun-loving.'
See Baby drop his toy car. He says, 'Fuck'
[New word], copying Mummy when, her luck
Out, she drops a pan. Tim smiles. All's well.
Mummy doesn't. Some hope. Time will tell.

That's life. Dick's old chum Hamlet's off his head,
Finding his uncle's killed his dad to bed
His mum. See Dick fall down in his own sick.

I've not forgotten Fluff, even if Dick
And Dora have. Cats have nine lives, but how
Each flashes past. Fluff would be dead by now.
But sixteen years ago, in fact one day
Later, Fluff met a fox. She tried to play.
'Mee-o' was mown short. See Fluff's flying fur.
It didn't feel so quick a death to her.

For Dick and Dora still what, if they knew it
Was coming at them, neither would go through it.
They do not see yet cancer, madness, heart
Disease; past cure [new experience]; each fresh start
Mocked by its outcome; then the vortex fear
Of age; still worse, what dulls that, close and near.

No fun. Meanwhile, see Dick gazing down
Into the river where the summer town,
Is mirrored, houses, shop-fronts, trees, intact,
Inverted and at peace. Waters refract
To purity the spoiled, soured life we've got.
Dick knows he'd drown there. Wishes he did not.
He thrashes it with a stick, and sets it shaking,
Until the globe of the lost world falls, breaking.

Flax Dams in Country Derry

Remember? – twilight thrilling
With birdsong as we trod
The scented path that wound
Past gleaming sheets of water
Configured as if a timeless natural feature
To the slopes; and glad,
Our welling hearts attuned.

Wherein a slow fermenting –
As when green flax in sheaves
Weighted by stones is sunk
Until the outer woody
Husk is loosened – had through weeks already
Disclosed the core, and love's
Unstinting urge to thank.

Fish set the surface trembling;
Along a plank we balanced
Over the sluice, then down.
To find numb petrifaction:
The linen factory's stark dereliction;
Stilled waterwheel, sheds silenced;
Tramlines half-overgrown.

Not living, yet not buried.
As circumstance, claims, fear,
Which from the shadows mutter
Would leave what in each other's
Arms we know. That may, transfiguring either's
Pasts, bring us once more
Unwearied to moving water.

Might Have Been

Your showpiece garden: sweeps of blossom, flowing
Brook, beguiling vistas. I try scents
You name, and call them lovely – and you, knowing
Me ignorant, think it indifference.

But in my heart from childhood still there burn
Dense purple spikes of lost delphinium;
Vermilion clumps of clustered phlox return
Fragrance like love's pulse to strike me dumb.

And when at talk of art or science thought
Turns to all in me left uncultivated,
It forms to vivid blooms, wraiths not of what
Took place, but things untended. Or unfated.

In Memoriam Dermot Nolan

1913-1992

Midnight, more falls of rain on deluged ground
Ambush my thoughts with the image of that place
Where you lie cold, the branches' whip and sigh
Comes desolately to me as its trees' sound.
I never called you father to your face,
Father. Adopted at six days old, I
Was forty when we met, your hand thrust in
My own was my first clasp from any kin.

Ex-military, tidy about your flat,
Your boisterous laugh and balding head were mine;
Buoyant you gripped the car-wheel, shirtsleeves rolled;
Leapt from a summer bank we picnicked at
To cleave the Thames. Till round your slow decline
Horizons shrank. Room, corridor, your old
Friends dead, 'must be put up with'. In that plot
Of earth stiff at your sides now void hands rot.

I stood dark-suited in the Abbey where
Candles flickered, tinkling censers swung.
Some of the mourners knew me, from your club;
Others learned with surprise why I was there.
I listened to talk of you when you were young,
Escapades, inventions. At the hub
Of ravelling grave ceremonial,
I watched you sunk as rain began to fall.

Hours sorting papers, photos, medals, books –
You'd willed me everything, unguessed by me.
Emptying your wallet felt almost a theft.
Now views you knew hang from my picture hooks –
Your College; Burma. You'd be glad to see
My son with the binoculars you left.
Your grandchild, Dermot. Still the drenched boughs sob;
But new by sodden roots fresh snowdrops bob.

The Self-Seeing

> *Blessings emblazoned that day;*
> *Everything glowed with a gleam;*
> *Yet we were looking away.*
>   Thomas Hardy, 'The Self-Unseeing'

What we walked into didn't just begin
When we reached, beyond the edge of town, the windmill, white
Sails motionless; already among the cobbled tight-
    packed streets, half-timbered houses painted in

Lime and ginger dozing in the light,
Something within us had been burnished. Leisurely
The incline elevated us to sight of sea
    On both sides of the island. At the height

Of the 'Ærø Alps' – as they term seventy
Metres – we ate our picnic, near the standing stone
Commemorating the union under the Danish crown
    Of these long grasses, place-names suffixed 'by'.

At Tranderup we checked the map, turned down
Towards the coast. Occasional white farms, thatched or tiled,
Embraced three sides of courts where bales of hay were piled;
    Lanes looped round unreaped ryefields' rippling brown.

Opening another cola, you said, my child,
'I think this is the happiest day of my life.' The thing
Most miss is knowing it while it's still happening –
    Not just in hindsight, maybe then beguiled

By tricks of the mind's lens that time's gulfs bring.
Along the strand I watched calm sunlit waters sway:
This was the Baltic yet I felt, so far away
    From home, a validating homecoming.

A couple of hours' stroll back, and then we'd play
Crazy golf, perhaps in the town square admire
The old pumps, hollyhocks, the church's needle spire.
    I said just, 'It's not yet late in the day.'

Two Chapters of an Old Natural History

Above the level of the ocean and
Defended against its irruptions, land,

> The rhinoceros is very large
> And strong. This quadruped
> Has skin insensitive to flies
> In thick folds. It is said

Enamelled with flowers, adorned with verdure which
Always renews itself, above all rich

> That in old Roman spectacles
> It fought elephants. Certainly
> The one the French King sent the Pope
> Destroyed its ship at sea.

In numberless species of animals, is a place
Of perfect repose. Upon this good Earth's face

> He bears his weapon of offence,
> A hard horn, on his nose.
> His limbs are massy, his large feet
> Each armed with three great toes.

In its delightful habitation, Man
Presides, his destiny to aid the plan

> He feeds on grossest herbs and shrubs,
> Resists muskets, spears. His brain
> Is small. Rash, without sentiment,
> He is no use until slain.

Of Nature, over all other beings. He
Alone possesses the capacity

> His skin makes leather, and the flesh
> Some reckon excellent,
> While esteemed remedies are made
> From horn, blood, excrement.

For knowledge, dignified in his prime station
By the faculty of admiration.

Two Views of the Whale

1 FROM A MEDIEVAL BESTIARY

Cethegrande is a fish,
Largest in water that there is;
Seeing one, you'd say it must stand
Like an island on the sea-floor's sand.
When this huge fish is hungry, he
Gapes his mouth wide in the sea,
And from his throat comes forth a breath
That is the sweetest thing on earth.
Charmed by it, other fishes swim
Into his mouth, so drawn to him
Float ignorant of his trick, till sucked
Within as the whale's jaws are locked.
This fish dwells down at the sea's ground,
And lives there, ever hale and sound,
Till times when storms stir the whole sea,
When winter strives for victory
With summer, when rising, he floats still
While the weather is so ill.
Ships, scattering as the seas drive,
Fearing death, longing to survive,
Looking around suppose this fish
The island for which they all wish;
So the rejoicing sailors steer
To it, use all their strength, draw near,
Fasten their ships, go up, with tinder
Make a fire blaze on this wonder,
Warm themselves, and eat and drink.
He feels the fire, and starts to sink,
Diving at once to the sea-ground
He kills them with no wounds, all drowned.

Whoever attends the devil's lore
In time shall rue it, that is sure;
Whoever fastens hope on him
Shall follow to hell's regions dim.

The order *Cetacea*, large marine
Animals, is divided into two
Groups, those possessing teeth, and the baleen
Whales which eat by straining plankton through

Horny plates inside the mouth. Some dive
For over an hour, to surface spouting air
Through blowholes in their heads. Most types survive,
Though vastly reduced in numbers everywhere.

Social behaviour. Living in schools, the whales
Often move in ballet-like formations.
They help their sick. Grown calves, when something ails
Them, seek their mothers. Seasonal migrations

Cross many latitudes. They like to play,
Leaping and riding waves in aerobatic
Antics; pitchpoling on their flippers, grey
Whales rise to look around them. These aquatic

Creatures have evolved a complex mix
Of sounds, enabling communication
Over huge distances: barks, whistles, clicks;
Use sonar echoes to aid navigation.

Whaling. Guns fire the harpoons, and a fuse
Explodes the charge. The carcass is inflated,
Left to float flag-marked while the ship pursues
Others. Processing is facilitated

By flush deck-openings on factory ships
Which in less than an hour can dispose
Of a 100-ton whale. Machinery strips
The blubber, bone is cut up. Nothing goes

To waste. The flesh we shun makes cattle-feed,
The cooked bone bone-meal; oil yields margarine,
Varnish, soaps, lubricants, things people need
From cosmetics to commercial glycerine.

Natural Justice

'I've marshalled you, marsupials,
    For just war! Kangaroos,'
Says the Koala, 'it appals
    You that the humans use
Your skins for making cuddly toys
Of – *us*!' Tails thump, a thunderous noise.

'And gentle wombats, for their crops'
    Sake, you expire in traps.
This New Year Day oppression stops!'
    Guns pouched, his audience claps.
Bikes rev, they vroom across the brown
Scrubland into the drowsy town.

They zoom through supermarkets wrecking
    Shelves, zap shoppers, batter
Machines, canteens, do wheelies decking
    Cops, rip skirts, shirts, scatter
Cricket from wickets. The mayor's worst fears
Take shape: blob noses, furry ears.

From wallaby wallops, kanga cuffs,
    Folk reel, the hind-feet shocker
Rends ribs; but the most vicious stuff's
    The whopper from the quokka;
While wombats snarling 'Who wants trouble?'
Kick civic statuary to rubble.

'They're stuffed, enough, we've done our duty,
    But shun extermination!'
Horns blaring, bearing looted booty,
    They roar in neat formation,
Singing 'Triumph to the Just!'
To vanish through the summer dust.

The Cheetah

So here they are, what above all
    You've longed to see – the cheetahs.
Earth's swiftest beast, its speed exceeds
    One hundred kilometres

An hour. They lope or laze, strong tails
    For turning in mid-chase
Twitch idly. Born to run, they know
    It's pointless in this place.

One briefly scampers at a trot
    To hint what it might do;
From instinct cubs play stalking games
    Though born inside this zoo.

Another pads to the wire-mesh,
    Pauses. Eyes meet. We see
Crisp rippling sandy fur, black spots,
    He views us patiently,

Neither as prey, nor threat; has seen
    So often the likes of us.
Our camera clicks, he flicks away.
    And we go for our bus.

When in your sleep's wide plains a gold
    Streak veers, coils, springs, eyes slits,
Is it the cheetah treads your dream,
    Or you who've entered its?

Annie's Cats

You don't want to think of them too
soppily – or take them too lightly.
      Gavin Ewart

'Misty' because it was after that misty day
On our visit to Lincoln, trees like iron hung
With waterdrops that did not drop, you chose
    Her, and her long fur was grey;
Her sister, runt of the litter, was black: 'poor Mel'.
Eighteen months ago, and I would tell
    Of your cats, who died so young,
Appropriately, indeed not scanting those
Small lives, nor mawkishly embalming them
In large words they can't fit. Yet I would cherish them.

For memory is mother of the Muses, and
The impulse to preserve root of all art,
Which though it cannot make amends for what
    Life voids, by troubling to understand
How it was, what happened, taking pains
Composes what through shapeliness sustains
    Truths that every bleeding heart
Hungers homeward to. So let me not
Fear relaxing to fidelity, to sprawl
Languorous, humdrum, attentive, as cats relaxing sprawl.

Romping together, Misty and Mel would rise
Like porpoises, turn hairpin bends in chase,
Climb curtains, wallpaper, then flaked out flop
    Together, paws entwined, shut eyes,
Upon the fireside rug or kitchen floor.   .
And your huge garden all theirs to explore.
    It seemed they owned the place.
Bold Misty scrambled trees, patrolled atop
The roof. It was poor Mel could not get down –
You'd fetch the ladder... They pranced at snowflakes fluttering
    down.

But if cats have nine lives, as spring came on
These seemed to flicker past. It was Misty fell
Into your brook, discovered she could swim.
    But the black kitten was set upon
By something in the night which gouged her lip;
Dragged when you slammed your car door shut to clip
    Her tail. Always poor Mel,
Who had no purr, seemed risking life and limb.
But it was her sister who disappeared.
One May evening Misty simply disappeared.

Run over? Stolen for her chocolate-box
Feline good looks? Of course, you called and searched,
Asked around neighbouring farms. Mel miaowed, bereft.
    Was Misty cornered by a fox?
You flinched at thought of that. But never heard.
Days became weeks, and neither corpse nor word . . .
    And Mel still moping, perched
On the wall, bewildered only she was left . . .
You kept Mel in at nights now, and she slept
On your bed, sucking your duvet-cover as you slept.

And yet, in time, in truth, it turned out that
Misty's death, her dominant role gone,
And having only you to play with now,
    Turned Mel into a supercat.
They say cats only haunt round one for food –
Mel, you'd swear, was attuned to every mood
    You had; when you were on
The phone, would sense your joys and sorrows. How
She loved to hide and seek, crouch, rush and spring
Dabbing your cheek, claws sheathed . . . So, summer bloomed
        from spring.

Each night your doorstep call, clear as a bell,
And from the orchard, or from fields away,
You'd hear her *miaow* race nearer, through the grass,
    And leap forth, green eyes luminous – Mel!
Until she didn't. Echoing through the night
Your cries; you scoured the garden at first light,
    Sat helplessly to pray . . .
'Just an animal,' they say, 'your pain will pass.'

You found Mel at the foot of your long drive,
Hit by some unknown person enjoying a late drive.

We guessed she had been coming to your call
Across the Kilrea Road, where she would roam
After field-mice, rabbits (cats kill too).
    Unsquashed, unmarked, she'd managed to crawl
To the verge, put paw to her hurt head, and died.
You clutched her stiff corpse to your breast, and cried.
    And so brought poor Mel home.
A strange thing: her green eyes had turned pure blue.
After which, you vowed to have no cats.
And then decided yes, you would get two more cats.

I must digress, to a cemetery far away
From Mel in your Derry orchard. For her death
Coincided with my own more wrenching grief,
    My father's death. That rainy day
We watched him lowered into earth in Ealing
Mel flashed into my mind, and I stood feeling
    (Dad there, no pulse, words, breath,
My heart half-exiled from the priest's belief),
It wrong to overlap two planes of loss.
Then, no: no prim excluding thoughts belong to loss.

Then something strange again, when as chance brought
Us down a London street that I'd last walked
'Thirty years back,' I told you, still the same
    Big bough-wreathed houses, and I thought
Of Chloe Stallibrass, who'd lived in one,
Pictured her bubbly hair and sense of fun,
    You said (and we'd not talked
Of kittens), 'I know what I'm going to name
One of my cats – Chloe.' Coincidence?
Consider the odds: it seemed more than coincidence.

And there's the fact that I, but only I,
Knew that rare name was flickering in my mind;
And it happened in that street. I can't explain.
    Telepathy? And if so, why?
Things happen, and it's maybe better not
Knowing, before they ambush you, just what...

It didn't take long to find
Chloe and Megan. So, you'd start again.
You brought them round. Tabbyish-grey, and weak,
Chloe's life-adventure had entered its fourth week.

You took her home. She vomited and shook.
You couldn't bring her round from kitten-'flu.
The vet said, 'She's too little to get well.
    Just squeeze her, gently.' But it took
Most of the night. You buried her small frame
Next to Mel. So Chloe left a name
    Into which she never grew
For a successor, little tortoiseshell
Chloe II – you took another chance.
She too fell ill, it looked as if she had no chance.

You spooned in medicine; she couldn't keep
Food down; hour after hour she just lay dazed
On a hot-water bottle . . . Megan would chase
    A pine-cone, climb, or burrow deep
Into your linen-basket. She was black,
Short fur a silken gloss along her back,
    But the white dash that blazed
Upon her throat below the pudgy face
Gave her a clerical air . . . There came the day
Chloe pounced for the cone. And throve after that day.

Soon Chloe was the bigger of the pair,
Ousting timid Megan from your lap.
At my house (not, like yours, a bungalow)
    Chloe would preen on a high stair
Then *mi-mi-miaow* her friend to playful fight.
Fun and games that lasted till the night
    That you felt something flap
Against your car's back wheel as cornering slow
You parked at your front door. You got out, saw it:
Megan, head crushed, eyes bulged forth. Chloe never saw it.

But in the morning, as you hosed away
The clotted blood, Chloe came, smelt, and howled.
The guilt you felt for what you'd never meant!
    For many weeks Chloe would not stray

44

From your patio. Those who would have us believe
It sentimental to think dumb beasts can grieve
    Don't know how Chloe yowled
For weeks. Not human loss, but evident
Loss . . . So once more, just one: Chloe (II).
She's made it to six months, is happy again too.

I watch her flicking eyes and winking ears
Beseeching us to play. She trails you round
Each time you dig or weed, in rainstorms too.
    And tentative from your pond's edge peers
At huge fish gorging on frogs' new-laid spawn.
She reposes on your sofa, or at dawn
    The bird-table. You found
She'd hidden bones you gave her in a shoe.
As you caress Chloe's black-white-caramel
Fur, you still assert 'There's no-one like poor Mel!'

Cats, as well as humans, can haunt our dreams.
Last night, for instance, after much ado,
A restaurant, us with friends around a table;
    And Misty cavorted, shredding reams
Of paper. And suddenly through the open door
A great white stag swept in, I watched it gore
    The kitten, ripping through
Her stomach . . . She wriggled, best as she was able,
Towards us (you'd not noticed), mortally hurt.
I woke crying 'Annie! Annie! it's Misty, she's so hurt!'

Well, likely enough, while writing this, I should dream
Of cats. And death. It's an eventful tale,
But where's the grand design, or even plot?
    Sheer melodrama with no theme,
Except this lesson: that love cannot save
What's colonised its orchard grave by grave;
    That our lives, too, are frail,
Perishable as our pets', and not
Only in newsfilm wars. As now you ring me
To tell of your relative's death, and once more wring me.

*

45

Two years have passed. Your garden blooms again.
Again two cats at play. Not Chloe, who
Last June lured by night's scents past the road's edge
    Was hit and killed. Again your pain;
Watched by, from the slab which you had laid
Over Chloe, her kitten Marmalade.
    Autumn came, cold winds blew,
Piteous, small, insistent, from a hedge
Cries brought you running. And so you discovered
Death-sick, dumped – Lillehammer. By your help he's recovered.

Evolution

Why do I linger to watch them dart and pass,
Brilliant slivers unfathomably repeating
Themselves, all they know on their aqueous side of the glass
Among wavering fronds is the throb of gills, and eating.

One speckled gold, with tail like a butterfly's wing;
Some hooped red white black; and there a serrated sail
Like something cut from black crêpe is hovering;
Others are lost in their lace of fins and tail.

There are paper-thin translucencies, filaments
Of life, yet every organ intact. So what
Evolutionary imperatives make sense
Of such miniature perfectedness? It cannot

Be for concealment, such consummate display
Must have to do with courtship; their purpose for ever
Is just to make more of themselves. I turn away,
Strolling back out to the city, where our clever

Species bustles among what it's erected
Since, fin-and-wing-less, perhaps a million years
Ago it rose staggeringly upright. Traffic-infected
Air corrodes churches, chainstores, concrete tiers

Of parking – ornately bizarre as our grandest conceit
Of what we are, politician, professor, priest, poet;
Our courtships riddled with notions of love that defeat
Its fruition; inventions destroying earth as we know it.

And wondering what in nature explains, I think
Of that phosphorescent violet fish that, turning,
Vanished edge-on then flashed again – like a wink
From depths of inscrutable creative yearning.

47

Animal Crackers

Through millions of years these things evolved
To do what then through millions more
They did as if they'd got life solved:

Natural selection meant what they did best
On the Cretaceous forest floor,
When not pausing for a rest,

Or sex, or to chomp dreary vegetation,
Was head-bang each other on the hop.
Generation on generation

Woke daily to more bouts of knockabout.
Pointless, but they couldn't stop.
Till naturally they died out.

We reckon a career like that would bore us:
I can't face up to that again. . . .
Micropachycephalosaurus

We've named them. Fancy title. All that's found
Is thick skulls with scant room for brain
For aeons fossilised underground.

The Frankish Merovingians popped their clogs,
Reign over because bred effete.
Now our Dark Ages ideologues

Of Literary Theory, who can't read or write
A real book, groggy on their feet,
Wield their dense texts in vain fight.

The Institution

He entered into the spirit of the project;
Served on the first committees, that established
A framework for promoting truth, the object.
    He was an idealist.

There'd be some power-corrupted, others hanging
Onto their forelocks for dear life, he realised;
And muddle's nets to check what we'd send winging.
    He was a realist.

The cat sat on the mat. The Council ruled
It was a dog on a log. There was some protest.
Many who saw differently were killed.
    He was an idealist:

'For Christ's sake, all we promised...' he implored.
'I'm not Christ,' said the Captain, unabashed,
'I cut my cloth...' He fled the whirling sword –
    He was a realist.

Quinquennial Plans, Personnel Development Schemes,
Bribes, marriage deals – the barbarians are vanquished.
Brilliant towers supplant forgotten dreams.
    He is an idealist.

From mountain caves with other exiles raiding
Wrecked libraries, condemned as terrorist
By those whose tumult is his safest hiding,
    He is a realist.

How Protestant Ulster Won the World Cup

We faced the whole menagerie, a mix
Of Papists, atheists, other heretics.
The Poles? Chopped. Dutch? Ditched. Cameroons? No hope,
Them darkies couldn't knock snow off a rope.
We played as in the bygone days of yore –
It wasn't sweepers or a flat back four
Won King Billy glory at the Boyne,
But thranness, strike-rate, crunching skull and groin.
Brazil in the quarter-final tried all tricks,
Backheels, swerves, dummies, one-twos, bicycle-kicks;
They'd not last one late night in Newtownards.
The ref was sprouting red and yellow cards.
Bookings, was it? – wee Sam fetched him a skelp
With the Good Book, you should have heard him yelp.
'No artistry, technique, footballing ideals,'
Carped critics, 'No coach, bar that wreck on wheels!'
Aye, we've no truck with such idolatries,
Newfangled texts, quare diets, shrinks, spin-off fees.
Fired up on the Ulster Fries we love,
The only sponsor we need's Him Above.
The semis was Germany. See Fritz's running
Off the ball, us in pursuit! He's cunning:
Dives in the box, greetins and girnins, till
He'd conned a spot-kick, stroked it home: 1-0.
We upped our game. Now they weren't shamming dead.
Their goalie picked up, looked to throw – instead
Was hit by Billy going like a train
Clean through the net, we're back on terms again.
Penalty shoot-out. We'd trained using live
Rounds in the Mournes, no way Fritz could survive.
As the smoke cleared a staunch voice sounded from
The stand: 'Next time, we'll replay at the Somme!'
The media boys were cracking up, the Pope
Redd out the Vatican for a hank of rope.
Our team, in orange sashes, brave and broad,
Lined up to put the Spaniards to the sword.
The rest is history. Our names resound
From Strabane to Strangford, Erne to Rathlin Sound.
Them dancers pushed the ball round smooth as silk.

Big Willie John turns slower than the milk,
But he'd not give an inch. He dug a trench.
(There was some noise upon it from their bench).
See Jim's Jack Russell, Hughie's Kerry Blue,
They'd not be bluffing, took a limb or two.
We buried the Fenians; then the referee.
And lifted the World Cup in victory:
'Yousuns get back to your fancy hacienda –
What we have we hold, and no surrender!'

He raised it high again, swigged, jack-knifed, boked.
The barman said, 'The eejit's went and choked.'
The great Ref in the Sky had blown Offside;
His fantasy exploded as he died.
Yet through Infernal smoke he made out more
Who'd got the worlds they'd once been asking for:
Midas deranged by gold he couldn't spend;
Stalin patrolling gulags without end;
Romeo cursed with Juliet at his throat;
Academics doomed to read the stuff they wrote.
For him, a rain-swept divot, and the thrum
Of bigoted sermonising, Lambeg drum;
Great gales stentorian with ancient malice;
Still dead-weight on his lap the poisoned chalice.

For Pete's Sake

See him. He's a bluffer. For Pete's sake,
That grimed black dented lump of a thing he drives,
Swilling red wine – godfearing motorists make
For the gutter, veer down turns, scared for their lives.

Pete's field was astrophysics, till he took
Up litigation, for a laugh. He mastered,
And set up judging, all crimes in the book,
Most punitive when manifestly plastered.

'Nil carborundum illegitimi'
He crows, grinding the bastards – me and you.
No earthly mandate for his tyranny,
Just signs and wonders, tricks out of the blue.

We try debate, try pleading, not a word
Comes back – just carnage, heartbreak, wars, disease.
It's no go Einstein, or a trip to Lourdes,
He'll still cut off your balls for his deep freeze.

He's toying with us, winds us up, may wind
Us up the other way as a mistake
He's bored with. Playing God. Out of his mind.
Or ours, whose need dreams him up, for Pete's sake.

Anne Frank's House

It is easily overlooked, one in a row
Of narrow elegant houses along the canal;
So we walked past it, as fifty years ago
    Der Militar at nightfall.

But certain of what we were looking for
Asked and retraced our path, so came to stop
As millions now do annually at the door
    Where you hid, off the map.

We paid, climbed narrow stairs, and filtered round
The revolving bookcase: your 'Secret Annexe'. So,
Here you ate, studied; tiptoeing so no sound
    Reached the warehouse below.

Pinned still upon a wall is your 'film-star
Collection'. Valentino, Garbo, smiles
Frozen in time. Like yours on the brochure.
    And your diary tells

How at night your fingers pulled aside
The curtain, past reflections on the pane
You peered into darkness: air-raids, people dead,
    More Jews crammed in the train

Of no return. *One can't get them out of one's mind.*
Yet, *we still have our jokes, and tease each other.*
You, the Van Daans, pompous Dussel, your kind
    Father, prim sister and mother.

Careful. Pencil markings here record
Your growing. For a while. Wherein you muse
Of *when the war is over.* Your heart soared
    To catch joy as it flies.

Then it was over. Abruptly you recede
Into lost millions. How does the spirit gloss
Belsen? *Who but myself will ever read
    These letters?* Anne, your voice

Speaks in all the world's tongues today. Your war
Is never over. In Bosnia, Ireland, though
Betrayed still your annotations refute all our
        Power to destroy.

And in each of us that secret annexe where
Something part child, part adult shelters thus,
Soliloquising; exiled from what out there
        Has gone dark and dangerous.

Towards the Light

I.m. Olive Waterman 29 June 1900 - 4 June 1994

I am told, 'You belong to darkness.'
Perhaps, perhaps, but I walk toward the light.
    Pablo Neruda

I was an airflight away –
On the phone they'd said you'd seemed better, drunk tea –
When my sister cradled your head as your breathing
And pulse expired. 'Mum,' she said,
'You didn't make it for the Mozart Players.'
    And the matron replied,
    'She's with Mozart now.'

Not in your book, you weren't.
Born with the century, one of the last
Victorians, 'ordinary Smiths' moving
In search of greenness, fresh air, light,
Down the Great Eastern Railway line:
    Bethnal Green, Cambridge Heath,
    London Fields, Hackney Downs,

The names 'a cruel joke'.
For that crowded, gaslit, horsedrawn world
Where the many toiled for a pittance, the few –
Well, you'd recall them waggling derisive
Cigars at your Mayday parades from affluent
    (Doomed, as you thought)
    Clubland balconies;

Or how, when one lay ill,
The streets were hushed with straw so that
The ailing plutocrat's repose
Might not be troubled by the traffic
Of ordinary folk. Your gospel
    Was socialism in
    Its unsullied dawn.

Uncle George inspired you,
Seeker after truth, and lover
Of Dickens, shelterer of roaming
International Workers of the World –
The 'Wobblies'. Out there at Enfield
    George also grew
    Fine strawberries,

And when, desirous to purchase,
With compliments and a fancy basket
The lady came, you waited giggling:
'You people think you can *buy anything*...!'
She received a sermon on Property is Theft –
    And the fruits of Uncle
    George's patch free.

Staying there at weekends,
You were woken at five o'clock: 'Are you coming?'
George, with wirecutters. You followed
Rejoicing in their voluptuous snip
Along the public paths of Cuffley,
    Keeping a bit
    Of England free.

Wearing your Sunday School badge
You told friends in sepulchral tones
Without a blush that its *IBRA*
(In fact *International Bible Readers'*
Association) meant *International*
    Brotherhood of
    Real Anarchists.

Those passionate meetings, discussions!
Keir Hardie speaking in Trafalgar Square,
Socials at the William Morris Centre,
Jim Larkin's Irish strike, suffragette marches...
At political street meetings your role
    Was reciting the poems
    Of Blake and Shelley,

Drawing a crowd around
(Unthinkable in our electioneering
Today), before making way on the soapbox
For the candidate's plea for a Just Society . . .
'Be good,' they warned, 'or the Kaiser will get you!' –
      His moustaches bristled
      From newspaper photographs.

      And when, in his war, believers
Refusing to slaughter their comrades, hid out
In Epping Forest, you brought them food;
At the party organised for them whirled
Them from arm to arm to the sound of music
      Till raiding police
      Joined in the dance.

      The huge airship enveloped
In searchlights passed above your house northward;
You saw it burst into flames, as fiery
Pieces floated to those fields round Cuffley
And the guns stopped, there was long silence;
      You stood in the garden
      In a ghost world.

      And across the blacked-out valley
At first a scatter of voices singing,
My home in Tennessee, That's where I long to be,
Till the whole suburb was rocking with sound,
And you turned indoors, and thought of the German
      Aviators burning
      To death in the sky.

      Uncle George was killed by the war.
Not in it. By it. 'Never the same'
After the air raid when fetching back tea
For the clippie who'd sought shelter from
Her abandoned bus met the blast. 'I put her
      There,' he'd repeat,
      'I put her there.'

Mother, the light you sought
Also meant music, the theatre, poetry.
Talented at the piano, on leaving
School you were told this pointed to
A promising career as a typist,
  And sent to work
  In a City office.

But acting was liberation,
Toller's *Masses and Man, Singing Jailbirds*
By Upton Sinclair. When, in the office
Of his Globe Theatre Leon M. Lion
Offered professional terms, you declined –
  To stay free to perform
  'Plays that meant something'.

And working for Gerald Gould,
Poet, critic, editor, socialist
(Though the sea-green carpet in the tall house
That 'looked poured, not laid' abruptly stopped
At the stairs up to the servants' attic),
  The light for a while
  Seemed within reach.

But then came a second war,
Your life took a different story, adopting
Me as the London pavements shook
From the guns at Dunkirk, and the world became
A different theatre, the old scripts,
  Hardie, Shaw, Blatchford,
  Forgotten irrelevance.

And where, on motorised highways,
Are the Clarion Cycling Clubs now? There are still
Great actors, musicians, poets; but most
You'd hoped would seek them prefer the *Sun*,
Sleaze, soaps, soccer – only the last
  Of which (you supported
  Spurs) you could cherish.

In the wider world still darkness,
The Soviet Union, whose birth seemed
A dawn, lies a dismembered ogre;
And names familiar to your childhood
As cockpits of strife, Bosnia, Serbia,
      Are back on the map
      As that again now.

      But the roundabout doesn't merely
Come round again. You lived to see
Nelson Mandela walk from the darkness
Of prison into the light of the Presidency...
Fearful things wouldn't shape well, 'Some hope!'
      You'd shruggingly say.
      Yes, mother: some hope.

      And you never gave up. In recent
Years, a regretful agnostic still playing
Piano at services in your Sheltered
Housing, hearing the vicar exhorting
Gratitude for a just society,
      You took him aside
      And sermonised thus:

      'You ought not to talk like that
These people are old, they are very gullible.'
Mother, you were the oldest present!
At ninety you spoke of a 'final ambition –
To see Thatcher out of Downing Street.'
      The day she resigned
      I phoned: 'So what next?'

      And always the actual light
And landscapes beneath it. I see you bending
Here in Ireland on that Antrim cliff-path,
Eagerly naming the wildflowers that
You hadn't 'seen in the Home Counties
      Since away back
      Before the Great War.'

In the CWS morgue
(Still true to the Co-op) when they drew
The curtain, I meant to affirm what you doubted:
Your life's meaning, diffusive and sure
As falling rain. But your corpse lay
    Pale, cold, a waxwork
    That wasn't a waxwork.

I hear you on your beloved
Brahms: 'So truthful and brave. In old age
Still at concerts I close my eyes,
And listen, and the music floods me,
I give myself, and feel I've come home.'
    Gently I touch
    Closed lids in the coffin.

I almost forgot: your gymnastics.
Not in recent years, toting that zimmerframe,
But all those medals you won long ago!
And, as you meet whatever it is
We all must surmount at last, I picture you
    Vaulting it, looking
    Back with a smile.

Freeze that image! But no,
Apt enough for an uplift ending
It is swallowed in the flood of things
Going on, like a sentimental trinket.
I catch myself, as news comes in
    Of this or that
    In politics,

Or spotting a concert on telly,
Reaching for the phone to tell you,
'What do you think of . . . ?' – 'Don't miss this . . .'
The dialling-tone sings into my ear
Like ripples of eternity. . . .
    That's all for now.
    I'll talk to you again.

Flying High

French-windows and a sort of patio,
Our glasses stood on flagstones half-neglected
By talk of how we fear the world will go.
'Eliot' – someone waving his *Collected* –
'Was wrong, it's bang, not whimper.' Ban the Bomb.
South Africa. The issues are all clear
This summer night, as trad jazz flickers from
Inside to lap the lights and darks of beer:
Love, love, O careless love . . .
Whose party is it? This rock-firm house scaled
To more capacious days, crowned high above
With green dome, parapet, a little railed
Platform from which, I imagine, some
Stargazing Victorian *paterfamilias*
Stared and saw all clear . . . A couple strum
Guitars, and insects glimmer as they pass
Among leaf-muffled light. And, 'It's a classic
Post-colonial mess, the Congo. Hell.'
'Our generation'll clear out that Jurassic
Crowd who've fucked the world up.' Time will tell.
The mag I've picked up flops apart at where,
Stripped to a loincloth, bound, Patrice Lumumba
The Congo's first elected premier,
Cowers towards his murder. 'Another number?' –
Delia gone, one more round, Delia gone . . .
Then I go, helmetless upon the pillion
Of someone's motor-scooter, roaring on
With whistling in my ears as a million
Streetlamps like an exploding supernova
Swoop past, a sense of destiny: I know
I'll write poems fit to kick their tables over.
Flying high. Over thirty years ago.

Postcards from Norfolk

Turning, the eye can hardly tease
   Out among all our path is banked to crest
The braided blue-green mutabilities
   Of land, creek, marsh, dune; yet finds rest
Strangely in flux, mud, saltings, rafts
   Of meadow with cattle ravelling;
     And far and wide
       The sailing craft's
White wings; and fluttering
   Close-up a red admiral that
Rich with light is pirouetting at
   My side.

Thrilling through all, the ceaseless song
   Of high birds; casually punctuated by
Patterings as of a brief shower along
   The grasses as breeze stirs; and by
The time we rise, from open sea
   Flooding the channel comes the tide;
     Brimmed and linked
      Waters from quay
To causeways; and to ride
   At last our ebb to sleep, the slow
Tinklings of mast and halyard, music so
   Distinct.

Yes, there are too many boats on the rivers and broads,
The one moored ahead last night just bristled with Germans,
Astern a careers development manager
Out of his element. Yet winding through reeds
And sedge, past mallards and coots and diving grebe,
And foliage adoring itself in water,
Like the great rooted windmills with stilled sails
And squared white windows we settle into a place
Indifferent to trafficking out of sight.
We take to a dawdling path along the margin,
On our other hand marsh sprinkled with wildflowers
And traversed by slow triangles of sail
Round the river's bend. My son stands motionless
As the heron he's recording in his notebook.
Here the impatient heart falls into place:
Nothing moves fast, no slope is difficult.
And languid under a huge sky all night,
Ignorant of its salty destiny
Water laps our hull . . . A sudden shiver
Whitens that willow, like mortality.

3 LUDHAM, ST CATHERINE'S CHURCH, THE ROOD SCREEN

For those who gave to make what's here,
Intricate carved wood, tracery,
Pinnacled buttresses, *in the year*
Of ower Lord God MCCCCLXXXXIII,

The middle rail of folded leaf
Is inscribed: *Pray for the sowle*
Of John and Cycyly his wyf
And *alle other . . .* Centuries roll

Over what this hammerbeam
Roof sequesters. Civil fights,
Broad-brims with the zealot's dream
To beat out Popery's stained lights.

Still clear the colouring of those
Depicted on the rood screen's base:
St Edmund, St Walstan, St Ambrose –
And here St Appolonia's face,

Patron of dentists, with drawn tooth
In forceps . . . Perpendicular
Stonework clinches fossil truth
Outflanked by video, motor car.

Empanelled dead saints gather dust,
With faith in means whereby they bless;
Yet swell me to what feels like trust,
Winging unsure of its address.

Counting the Cost

Thousands of people gathered, their thousands of candles,
At the fiftieth anniversary of the night
The 'Florence of the Elbe' was cindered to moonscape
Stashed with (some calculate) 40,000 corpses.

Today's Mayor of Dresden says, 'We did it first.'
So it was all right? But that's true too of Auschwitz...
The Duke of Kent represents us, with careful words
Confined to 'regrets', not saying 'sorry'.

Which 'would infuriate Bomber Command, who lost
55,000 of 120,000 aircrew.'
I've met them in Lincolnshire, old men, recollecting.
'The Nazis weren't beaten, we felt we were saving our
        groundtroops

Thousands of lives.' It is hard, computing morality...
'In the cellar we found', I follow her through subtitles,
'My family, the bodies burnt tiny. Just one
I could recognise, I remember crying, "Aunt Ilse!..."'

February 1995

Death's Embassies

A stile. Wide light on slaking
   Greenness, silver thread
Of river, a deciduous slope. Heartbreaking
   Peacefulness outspread.

Thirty years ago. And no backtracking
   Could find what's leavened to
Pure image irradiating all that's lacking
   In things passed through.

Like others in me claiming
   Terrain, immunity
From temporal laws, demesnes we flinch from naming,
   This is death's embassy.

The flag proclaims though earthed in our condition
   They represent a power
Beyond it, colonising all cognition
   Each living hour.

THE END OF THE PIER SHOW

The Last Resort

When I sauntered along here the beach was emptied,
The roundabouts stilled, the lightless helter-skelter
Defrocked of shrills and skirls. Just one last boy
Running in vain to lift his flagging kite

From sand where a billion bubbles broke each instant
In the lacy fringe of an idling tide dissolving
Abandoned ramparts and keeps. It was the hour
When you were all back in your guesthouses and hotels,

Caravans and bars, or the crab restaurants.
And past the pier, low-slung by the cliff the sun
Stood on the sea a great red ball, so beautiful
I turned back for my camera... Only by then

It wasn't the same. Well, isn't that always the way?
And a shiver in the wind, but that might be rain...
Still, lovely to see so many of you have made it,
Especially the kiddies. This is a family show,

And it's warm in here, balanced above the heartstopping
Swirl underneath. A bit of a last resort?
Lady, d'you think I chose it myself? But nothing
Beats a good laugh. Don't laugh, you'll bring down the house.

Bygones

The microwaves are pinging in
The sidelanes where our mothers'
Greasy fingers plucked forth chips
From newsprint, while their brothers'
Pennies conjured saucy scenes
From *What the Butler Saw* machines.

Postwar Paradise, they'd cleared
The barbed-wire off the beaches;
Trawling shoals of seafront girls,
Permed, pencil-skirted peaches.
Golden lads and girls all must
Like Punch and Judy bite the dust.

Swept from the pier the Gypsy Seer,
The Crazy Mirrors Hall
Where Brenda burgeoned to blancmange
And Little Tich walked tall.
In Funland's din a high-tech toy
Chirrups Beethoven's *Ode to Joy*.

Skins then velvet to the touch,
Lips fluttering back when kissed,
Have long worn others to the bone,
But what you've had's not missed.
The show goes on, the lost heart eats a
Machine-tooled burger, plastic pizza.

Something for Everyone

Lifers on parole we deck ourselves
In primary colours, lapse to cleansing play;
Radios natter on hot sand that shelves
To ocean spread like harpstrings in the sun;
A cliff path dawdles round to the next bay.
Nothing so right, something for everyone.

Some bob in white at tennis, others steer
Gokarts hurtling round a tarmac 8;
Boat-trips, teashops, anglers on the pier;
A straggle on the stepped path up the East Hill
To the Smugglers' Caves. Some just contemplate
The goings-on, for once free to stand still.

From a beach kick-around, shirts for goals, the ball
Soars gloriously into a trajectory
That could clear the planet. Children call
Excitedly finding crabs, seeing the boat
Pirouetting. As we do, nonchalantly
By something in the ambience kept afloat,

As by a membrane beyond our discerning
Insects stroll water surfaces at will.
Here at the crazy golf we gauge the turning
Of a miniature windmill's sails that block or free
Path to the hole, knowing it's faith, not skill,
Freaks us through and on to victory.

A pointless game? Not quite. Of course that ball's
Dropped back to earth for kicking round in vain
Quest for perfection; a toddler's ice-cream falls
Splat on the pavement, and his sobbing rends
Our fragile harmonies – nothing can explain
Things will come right, the world will make amends,

Until the replacement is in his hands; and he
Must learn the further lesson as he grows:
Some things gone wrong have no such remedy.
Yet he'll come back, cliff-walking, bathing, fishing,
Drawn by the place's gift of, we suppose,
Immersion in a mutual well-wishing.

Rouge et Noir

The music starts, bring on the girls,
With tutus, laundered smiles, leg-kickings, twirls
In synchronised formation, just for you,
    The punters. Taut flesh out of reach
And lovelier than any on the beach.
None of this thrusting groin and breast seems crude
    Transfigured under lights into
    Family fare, an anodyne
        Signalling that life's fine:
You clap and clap in candid gratitude.

    Offstage, she drifts anonymous
Through supermarkets, hesitates from a bus
Between the pub and the swarmed-over sand,
    Indifferent. Inside her head
The awakenings: again a stranger's bed,
Their touching flesh, the glare of a new day,
    As to her cheek he reached a hand
    Her eyes stampeding to blank wall;
        And her mother's words from all
The spent years, *Child, don't wish your youth away.*

Double Trouble

As I walked on the beach this morning the voice
Arrested me, spinning me round.
'It is you!' he said. Lap lap lap went the waves.

Of course I remembered the face, from shaving mirrors,
In the Underground reflected across
The carriage brooding beneath thick hair, those eyes
Now bitter to find me bitter here
Between the dunes and the fluctuating breakers.
So I waited for what he must say, a drift
Of sand creeping over the distance between us.

'You have betrayed me, are all
I vowed never to be, why do you come,
Intruder in my perfect vista?'

'Because it was I was betrayed by you,
Here, or somewhere like here.
Your ideals still spin in my hurt head.'

'Divorcé, seller-out, wage-slave, clown,
You should never have been born.'

'You fathered me.'

Or was it this place, or others like it,
Generating hunger for distant brightness
That sears like betrayal now.

'Your worst sin against me is unhappiness.'

'Yours, thinking it only lasting for others.'

So I faced his intolerant virgin stare,
Till a sudden misting parted us – his cry
Inviolable to my stumbling forgiveness.

State of the Nation

In the very posh School on the headland where they wear
Different ties for Full Colours, Half Colours, Prefects
(Senior and Junior), House, and each year the Combined
Cadet Force marches to honour the Tudor Founder
Behind the Corps of Drums playing 'Men of Harlech'
and 'Sweet Polly Oliver', now in the chemistry classroom
Dr Dabby is demonstrating. He's Persian,
'Rub-a-dub-dub,' he utters, and 'Hubble-de-bubble',
According to him talking English, the boys all giggle,
'Abracadabra' – the whole bloody place explodes.
    'We are sorry to lose Dr Dabby,'
Says the Headmaster at end of term assembly.
'We sing now, as always, "Schola Quam Amamus".'

In the very Grand Clifftop Hotel old Spavin is tickling
The ivories, much as he has for a million years
Since the good old Edwardian days when top-hats and tiaras
Rolled up in carriages, talking of golf, horses, angling.
Now over Chili con Carne and Breaded Scampi,
Its 'globalisation' and 'accessing information',
They think they are talking English, none being aware,
As Spavin forsakes 'Tea for Two' for 'Ain't Misbehavin'',
That Hitchcock upstairs is accessing his PA's bed,
In he plunges – the whole bloody place drops into the sea.
    'We are sorry to lose the Grand Clifftop,'
Says the Mayor, 'But that's how things go with coastal erosion.'
The piano washes ashore at the Muppets' Paddling Pool.

In the very High Court Sir John (Mr Justice) Lately
Is flouting a welfare report by preventing a father
From seeing his son, the mother not wishing such 'contact'.
Not that he gives a bugger, red-carpeted round the circuit,
On huge pay and holidays, it's hardly surprising
His own kids don't see him, and after Court it's not homeward
He toddles, but off to the Club for a nap and a bottle.
In front of him now, one Counsel's asserting, 'It's chalk,'
The other, 'It's cheese,' he savours this travesty till,
'Just look in the bloody fridge!' – and the dad shoots him dead.
    'We are sorry to lose the old Judge,'

Say women he thought fit for nothing but minding the children,
And the one in the brothel who flogged him dressed as a schoolgirl.

On this very old Pier you can fish and eat candy-floss,
Riding the bumper-cars target the girl with huge knockers,
Go boss-eyed at the wheel of road racing simulator
Machines in Funland, or hanging your face through effigies'
Head-holes be photographed as a clown or gorilla;
Or sit writing postcards over your coffee, or saunter
The boards to the end, where our lifeboat is housed – yes, touch it.
Then come to the show. Traditions that run through the town
Story like lettering through rock. Until the Big Storm
Hurls a barge – clean through the ramshackle bloody structure.
    'We are sorry to lose the old Pier,'
The Town Council say, 'But the cost of repair, we must move
With the times, sell it off.' For one pound, or the nearest bidder.

Saussure and Lawrence: In the Oceanview Lounge

How dare you, sir, whoever you may be?
Though nothing you can say denotes reality.
I'm Bertie Lawrence, I got in my shout
Before you, the barman grasps what that's about.
Language is a matter of interrelations
Working through negative differentiations,
This furry creature on the stool is designated cat
Because the system dictates not dog, snake, bat.
> **How dare he, sir, whoever he may be?**
> **Though nothing he can say denotes reality.**

You should dip your toe, you bloodless linguistician,
Into the ocean of our human condition.
In the beginning was the Word,
It's the Book of Life. *Don't be absurd!*
Name-calling cannot touch me, if you believe
Words relate to objects you are merely naive.
My dad was a miner, when he knocked his head
On a rock 'I can't say a thing' wasn't what he said.
> **He should dip his toe, the bloodless linguistician,**
> **Into the ocean of our human condition.**

And if nowt means owt, you needn't duck or run
On being told this fist's about to dot you one,
Nor put up your own, so just sup your beer
And try differentiating cauliflower ear
From bloodied nose, I'm not so puddled with booze
That I cannot deconstruct you. *Pray excuse*
Me, I've suddenly recalled I've somewhere else to be.
That's seen him off. Now a swim in the sea.
> **And if nowt means owt, he needn't duck or run**
> **On being told this fist's about to dot him one.**

The Whole Thing

Like cloud-arms on the ocean
The lambent headlands lie;
Full waters' slumbering motion
Glitters beneath wide sky,
And any sigh
Of air breathes as devotion.

At ease from indecision
A sprinkling of moored hulls,
And muted the derision
Of interweaving gulls,
Nothing annuls
Intactness of the vision.

Never perhaps known better
Than when encountered first:
A birthright entered. Yet a
Reprise, the bubble's burst,
Something dispersed
From spirit, if not letter.

The Good Old Days

In the days of yore when the grass was greener,
And Britain ruled the waves and there'd never been a
    Drugging or a mugging,
    Nor a telephone-bugging,
Life was one long knees-up round a concertina.

Demob heroes of impeccable demeanour
Never lost at football to Brazil or Argentina;
    A Brisbane sticky wicket
    Was for Hutton just the ticket;
All was hunky-dory, and glory to the gleaner.

Sauntering pier and esplanade, pavilion or marina,
Arm-in-arm your blarney'd charm barmaid or ballerina,
    Pre-Aids sex a box
    Of multiflavoured chocs,
Winnowing willing women like a randy window-cleaner.

But as horizons rolled away the soul of things grew meaner,
You never got to heaven in a Ford Cortina:
    It proved Cloud-Cuckooland,
    Half vicious and half bland,
The rich getting richer, the graffiti obscener.

As muzak silts the supermarket, mall and mezzanine a
Sense the ship is going down around you becomes keener,
    The Royal Family crashes,
    And we never win the Ashes –
No testosterone in the Test arena.

Biggles, Bambi, Mr Toad, Dick Barton, Thumbelina,
Are as buried as King Arthur, now blood drips from the screen, a
    Thing from outer space is
    Melting human faces,
And Robin Hood rewritten rapes the village sweet-sixteener.

A fading blaze, the good old days once lambent and serene, a
Memory-trick of brain or dick, as blood gets cold, shanks leaner;
    The writing on the wall
    Speeds your dying fall
To generations long inert beneath where grass grows greener.

Interval

Interval. The bar
Is open. Faces,
Hairdos and glasses,

And glasses filled
With light or dark
Slowly emptied.

Or take a turn
Outside, consider
The lit skein along

The shore, discrete boxes
Where they are saying
'I love you' or

'It's over' over
Laden tables,
Or talking football,

Arched by the stars'
Spindrift. The void.
Listen to it lapping

Beneath you, drop
A coin for luck
Through boards of the pier.

But there is the bell.
Finish your peanuts.
The show goes on.

All at Sea

Raised above the huddle of the town
It catches us on the turn, a grey tower jutting
As we look back over mudflats wondering
Why we are grown used to not attending,
Bent on our pursuits, gone for a song.

Set on its eminence with intent to crown
Our goings-on, it is enamoured of moonlight,
Awash among stars its freight
Of centuries: rood screen, tombs, the quiet
Dust of old yearnings, conflict of wrong and right.

That ancient tumult of faith, the smashings-out
Of stained glass, whelming terror of a damnation
Flickering fire through faults in the hill's green,
The chiaroscuro of righteous passion,
Ebbed to a more worldly deformation,

Prosperous, well-dressed, with no self-doubt
Unhinging doors shut tight upon the soul,
What shall I do to be – respectable?
Its only cry, its moral rule
Immune to love or reason as its style

In bonnets. Practical Victorians, who put
The tower to use, employed it as a lighthouse
Sweeping illumination across dark waters
So mariners should navigate safe course.
Till a modern structure was built for the purpose.

Now, clambering the rocks about its foot,
Or cresting the Big Wheel's apogee,
When we notice it at all it is not what we
Have come for: 'Picturesque', we merely say;
But suddenly out of our depth, moved out to sea.

Love Makes the World Go Round

You combed the beach, impetuous for
    The off – and backed a beauty
With all first love, keeping faith more
    From rapture than mere duty.

Alas, among dunes' treachery she
    Veered off – bribes, or dope?
Well, *Plenty more fish in the sea*
    You knew, still young in hope.

Next time out you put your shirt,
    Your house, on – sweet fuck all,
Lashing heels. You watched, deep-hurt,
    Folly's sandcastles fall.

A stayer: 'Often decked,' she says,
    'Still questing on for' – you.
Those others, husbands, hunks, quick lays,
    'All proved untrue.' Untrue?

'I feed upon your feelings.' Polite
    As ever, you demurred.
'Take so much more than I give.' One night
    She took off, her last word,

(As her dud emotional cheque bounced over
    The moon) over the moon,
Blood filling her cheeks, 'May you discover
    Someone worthier soon.'

You weighed things. Played the field. You tried
    The thoroughbreds, goers, needy;
The promising proved to have lied,
    The spiritual turned greedy.

But what of other punters who
    Quit with the first race,
Claiming, 'There'll just be always you,'
    And that the answering face

Will equally none other love,
   Swearing they'll not be parted,
When being grown-up, Heavens above!
   Has scarcely yet got started,

Most of its entries not yet met?
   Plainly fucking insane!
As shadows lengthen, see them get
   Scrambled by boredom, pain.

Hubris! – vowing so young to give up
   Falling in love for ever,
Sip to the dregs one cooling cup...
   Time shows they've not been clever.

But you, as tides flood in, ebb out,
   Are left now high and drier;
Though annual fresh limbs splash about
   Setting your heart on fire.

Of those in your age-range most by now,
   If not too dire, are hitched
(Unless fouled-up with griping how
   They've been abused and ditched).

What hurts you most on her U-turn
   Back to her married station
Is that she lacks the guts to spurn
   Pride's raft of rationalisation:

Her mind there fragrant as a drain,
   Perspicuous as fudge,
Deliberative as a weather-vane,
   And honest as a judge.

So, given all they say about
   Flogging a dead horse,
Why is it you're still turning out,
   Intent yet on the course?

Simply, loss, waste, cannot define us,
  Nor fallen hopes destroy men
Driven by thoughts like those in Heine's
  Ich stand in dunkeln Träumen:

> *Stood in a dark dream staring*
> *Upon your picture, I've*
> *Seen those lineaments, dearest,*
> *Come secretly alive.*

> *And on your lips there gathered*
> *A brilliant smile, upon*
> *Your eyes up-brimmed heart-sorrow*
> *In teardrops till they shone.*

> *Also my own tears flowing*
> *Down my cheeks I knew –*
> *And ah, I can't believe it,*
> *That I'm bereft of you.*

Ghost Train

Read me a story. *Once upon a time . . .*
Is it about a wolf or wicked witch?
Oh yes. Your favourites. Once upon a time . . .

Red Riding Hood came to the cottage, raised the latch,
Entered the cosy room. From the brass bed . . .
I know – big eyes, big ears . . . *But now we reach*

'Granny, what big teeth you have,' she said.
'The better to eat you with!' And with a leap . . .
Etcetera . . . So at last the wolf is dead.

Tell me another. Where the children tip
The witch in her gingerbread oven . . . *There you are,*
All's come right in the end. Now go to sleep . . .

It's different these days. *Less familiar,*
The shapes? The thing that's clumping in the attic?
The Mummy's Curse comes true – he won't flee far.

And look, stood on the dunes with a raised mattock . . .
It's thrilling, but my dreams . . . *And there's no getting*
Off. Being clever, brave or energetic

Cannot halt the skull-faced figure flitting
Through trees towards our hero, or assuage
Its venom . . . Till I put the book down, sweating . . .

All's changed again. *Yes, horror's left the page.*
It hangs like an infection in the air,
And in my heart. *Ah, now you've come of age.*

Famine wraiths. Dead babies. High-tech war.
No use to seek or hide from it. It calls
Wreathed in smiles – you're opening the door.

It's scattering its seed through wedding bells.
Tell me another . . . *Insidiously it kills;*
This is our colonist, our cancer cells . . .

Once you took ghost trains for their phantom thrills,
Jinking past shrieks and skulls, that flashlit ape
Harmlessly roaring, pleasurable chills,

Knowing the ticket returned you in good shape
Into sane light. But once upon a time . . .
You drew another, one way, no escape.

On the Beach

Sand between your toes
Again, as you bend
All's there in a flash,
Spread golden before you

Banking to groyne after groyne,
The hush of waves lapsing,
Trance of cumulus,
All yours.

Behind you, the wooden steps
Down which you've escaped
The cliff-top games
(After winning the egg and spoon race),

The chalets sunning
Along flowerbedded paths.
Each breakfast the summons
O what a beautiful morning

From the Hall's loudspeakers
Beneath the galleon flag,
O what a beautiful day.
It is, it is . . .

Let them get on with the Dads'
Knobbly Knees Competition;
You are no age,
And do not know you are happy,

Crouched at the pool
Where a crab, at your touch,
Buries itself
In the pith of that day

When fleetness of childhood
Graced feet you'd, as now,
Inch by inch rise from,
Year upon year.

Table for Two

Table for two. A souse
Of tonic lifts the ice
Tinkling against the rim.
'Here's to us!' we chime,
Our walk, our cliffs, our bay.
No doubts. Pasts past today.

A signal to the waiter:
We order. His eyes flicker
Across the table, our
White sequestered square
Strangely now mutated
Expanding, others seated

Rightful at laid places,
Old familiar faces
Toasting me, vowing love,
Each intimate and exclusive,
The hubbub ever loudening
As I see across the widening

Blankness between us you
Absorbed in faces too,
Intent on each at once
As if none before or since,
On shared scenes, bits of coast
I've been told about, or guessed,

And the waiter growing sombre,
'It's far more than the number
Booked for, we've no room.'
And I cried out as the dream
Voided, leaving you
Rinsed singular, strange, new.

Steps in Time

The Roman skimmed stones on this sea,
  Guarding the Saxon Shore.
England wasn't England then,
  But war was bloody war.
The Empire crumpled in its tide;
  He left, and came no more.

The Normans built their castle high
  To dominate the port.
Sieges came and went. Some tongues
  Were torn out, limbs lopped short.
Still generations passed on charms
  To ripen corn, cure wart.

And fished and fiddled, pastured herds,
  Mowed lea, played pitch and toss,
Their talk as local as their beer;
  What matter gain or loss
Abroad, to sins here shadowed by
  The Gibbet and the Cross?

The railways came. Then cars. Today
  The Visitors Centre Staff's
Run off its feet; kids smirk astride
  Dead cannons for photographs;
Though skimming stones, arcade machines,
  Beat Heritage junk for laughs.

Saussure and Lawrence: On the Helter-Skelter

I can't know what's out there, naming it helter-skelter
Means nothing at all about it, thinglessly
Words mean only because not other words
In a self-enclosed system working through negation.
What is it all about? What should I do?

Get out of that chair, off into the great unknown,
Pick up that what for convenience we'll name mat,
And mind the otherness of the steps as you climb.
Then launch yourself away into life's adventure,
Let me know what it feels like, tell me the truth.

But you don't understand. Consider the 8.25
Train from Geneva to Paris: the carriages change,
And the staff, it may not leave until 9, but remains
The 8.25 train, purely because of its place
In a timetable's structure. Likewise words in language.

But it got you to what we'll agree to call Paris.
How were its let's say women? Saussure, you told
All that before you died in 1913,
As I launched my book of life with *Sons and Lovers*.
Stop whittling, and push off – or are you just frit?

I, I, whoosh and I float on chaos plunged
In vortex tumbling now head over heels
Sea over sky whirling both under land
This void and nothing able to tell but words
How can I know what on earth is happening?

He's gone arse over tip, the mardy old loon . . . You called 'Help'.
Well, here I am, you spoke truly, are bruised. Now come
To my house, it is open to receive you, as language
Embraces phenomena, as my poem welcomed
That snake 'Come a guest, to drink at my water-trough'.

We Really Must Go

Disassemble the big dipper, shutter discos and arcades,
Pull a switch and watch the lights dim, listen as the music fades;

Drain the Dolphinarium, box the bandstands, little seafront train,
Fold the pitch-and-putt course up and store it safe from snow and
    rain;

Headlands, castle, are deflated, sandgrains vacuumed by the ton;
Finally we pull the plug beneath the sea, reel in the sun.

Yes, another season's over, time to pack and say goodbye.
Off you go, some fitter, others fatter, bathing snaps don't lie.

Cleansing swims and lobster dinners, scuba diving, cliff-face
    thrills,
Vulnerably you came asking simple cures to complex ills.

Love for many: moonlit romance; ties refreshed; that mega-fuck
Causing caravan meltdown. But for other seekers, no such luck:

Kev's primeval chat-up gambit's left him reeling from a punch;
At the pier-rail his mate Colin's heaving up his liquid lunch.

Minor keys of major feelings. Bless you all, we do our best,
And next year when we reopen, you'll return, renew the quest.

Things may not be what they once were, run down, tarted up,
    the most
Fanciable women jetting off to sundrenched Spanish coast.

Contents captioned, two quid entry, see his oilskins, boots,
    pipes, bed,
Harold Blaggs's cottage, lifeboatman supreme, three decades
    dead.

Captain Flynn's Performing Ducks are still recalled by some old
    dear,
Also Professor Narwhal's blindfold cycle-dive clean off the pier.

Some of you, before next summer, will have fallen off the twig;
Annually in the Rat and Trumpet shoulders shrug between each
swig:

'Poor old Woody, who'd have thought it?' 'He'd that fearsome
cough, had Tom,'
Eyeing a new generation's pushchairs storming down the Prom.

Theirs will be a world of shimmering screens, and no horizons
set,
Crouched at keyboards surfing superhighways of the Internet.

Strayed from designer-slaughter movies, cyberspace and leisure-
dromes,
Baffled they'll gawp at lacquering, dado, in leftover stately
homes.

Once upon a time you heaved aside a massive stone and saw
Creatures scurrying hither, thither, wondered what it was all for;

That's the way we carry on, we haven't got a bloody clue,
Knowledge vaster, travel faster, ignorant why we are, or who.

Whiskered Victorian geologists tapping fossils from these rocks
Thought that *homo* finally was pulling up his sapient socks,

Cracking the code, deciphering the scheme of things entire: one
more
Heave and reason would dispatch disease, crime, ignorance,
slums, war.

For there'll always be an England: Prussian, Kaffir, Chinee, Turk,
Learning the rules, aspirant, would fall in with Progress's great
work;

Playing the game. Like Admiral Wilson, umpiring the
submarine's
Advent: 'Underhand, unfair, and damned un-English!' By all
means

Laugh if you must, nobody else is. There's too much blood in this
  farce....
Yet the show goes on, each April posts fresh bills up, mows the
  grass,

Still our unforeseeing congregations stare into the flood
Cresting, breaking; drawn here purely by sweet habit of the
  blood.